Volume Six
by Choi Kyung-ah

English Adaptation
by Sarah Dyer

HAMBURG // LONDON // LOS ANGELES // TOKYO

Snow Drop Vol. 6
created by Choi Kyung-ah

Translation - Jennifer Hahm
English Adaptation - Sarah Dyer
Associate Editor - Suzanne Waldman
Retouch and Lettering - Riho Sakai
Production Artist - Vicente Rivera, Jr.
Cover Artist - Anna Kernbaum

Editor - Julie Taylor
Digital Imaging Manager - Chris Buford
Pre-Press Manager - Antonio DePietro
Production Managers - Jennifer Miller and Mutsumi Miyazaki
Art Director - Matt Alford
Managing Editor - Jill Freshney
VP of Production - Ron Klamert
President and C.O.O. - John Parker
Publisher and C.E.O. - Stuart Levy

A  Manga

TOKYOPOP Inc.
5900 Wilshire Blvd. Suite 2000
Los Angeles, CA 90036

E-mail: info@TOKYOPOP.com
Come visit us online at www.TOKYOPOP.com

ISBN: 1-59182-689-6

First TOKYOPOP printing: November 2004

10 9 8 7 6 5 4 3 2 1

Printed in the USA

Previously in

Snow Drop

As Hae-Gi and So-Na's love continues
to bloom, another ray of hope shines on
Hae-Gi's life when his mother returns
from her recent operation. However, not
everything is coming up roses: Hae-Gi is
blacklisted in the modeling industry and
So-Na tries to fight off an arranged
engagement! Meanwhile, Charles and
ever-jealous Sun-Mi team up to crush the
flowers of romance and get what they're
both after -- Hae-Gi!

HMM. WAS THAT A WOLF?

It's been 3 hours, 20 minutes (and 57 seconds) since they got to the haunted mansion.

THIS IS EXACTLY WHY I HATE YOU, SO-NA!!

BLAH BLAH BLAH

HOW CAN YOU BE SO CALM? AREN'T YOU SCARED? AREN'T YOU HUNGRY? WE DIDN'T EVEN EAT!

YOU'RE SO RUDE! AFTER I LENT YOU PAJAMAS AND MY TOOTHBRUSH, TOO!

IF YOU HATE IT HERE SO MUCH, THEN JUST LEAVE! THERE'S THE DOOR!

YOU LEAVE!!

He dragged us all here for their stupid contest to see who can stay in the haunted room.

For this I have to share a room with my enemy, Sun-Mi? And Ha-Da and Ko-Mo have to share a room, after what happened... Is he serious? And what's this "the loser is the winner's slave"?

What exactly is the point?!

This is really pissing me off.

AAAH!!

CALM DOWN!! IT'S ME!

WE'RE HAVING A PARTY! THERE'S NO REASON TO WASTE OUR YOUTHFUL YEARS SLEEPING! C'MON!

7

Looks more like a séance than a party...

THIS IS ALL THEY HAD FOR SALE HERE. NO REAL FOOD AT ALL

AND NOTHING TO DRINK BUT BEER... URGH, I'M SO HUNGRY.

LOOK AT ALL THIS JUNK!

THIS IS PATHETI

Damn. I'm just gonna drink 'til I fall asleep...

HAE-GI... WHAT'S UP WITH YOU TWO YOU LOOK SO SERIOUS. DID ANYTHING HAPPEN?

10

Suddenly... the mood turns glum.

DAMN.

I can't believe I have to pee now!! No way am I asking Sun-Mi to come with me. But I don't want to go alone!

Maybe I can hold it?

HEY, SO-NA, WANT TO COME WITH ME TO LOOK FOR FOOD? THIS ISN'T ENOUGH; WE'LL ALL STILL BE HUNGRY...

I'M PRETTY SURE I SAW A GROCERY STORE NEAR HERE...

Did he realize that I needed to... take a walk?

Perfect! I'll just run up to the room while he's gone.

Heheh.

14

WHAT?
SOMEONE
TOLD YOU
ABOUT IT?

YOU MEAN
YOU DIDN'T KNOW
ANYTHING ABOUT THIS
PLACE, AND YOU DRAGGED
US ALL HERE ANYWAY?
IT'S MORE THAN JUST
"BLEAK," HAE-GI! I CAN'T
BELIEVE YOU DID THIS
WITHOUT EVEN
TALKING
TO ME!

WELL,
IT ALL--

THIS
IS STUPID!

MOST OF
US CAN'T STAND
EACH OTHER, AND
YOU THOUGHT THIS
TRIP WOULD BE A
GOOD IDEA? WHAT
KIND OF BET DO YOU
HAVE WITH HWI-RIM
THAT YOU PULLED
SOMETHING
LIKE THIS?

WELL?
YOU MUST HAVE
SOME REASON!
WHAT IS IT?

But... you'll have to keep our deal a secret, Hae-Gi...

WELL?

IT'S NO BIG DEAL. JUST A LITTLE CONTEST WE'RE HAVING...

NO BIG DEAL?

THEN WHY DID YOU GUYS HAVE TO DRAG US ALL OUT HERE WITH YOU?

THERE MUST BE MORE TO IT THAN THAT!

CALM DOWN, SO-NA...

The truth is...Hwi-Rim wants to break up with me in front of you.

DON'T PATRONIZE ME!!

NOT WHEN YOU DON'T TRUST ME ENOUGH TO TELL ME WHAT'S GOING ON!

WHY ARE YOU GETTING SO UPTIGHT? CAN'T YOU JUST TRUST ME?

DON'T THINK THAT YOU CAN JUST DO WHATEVER YOU WANT, JUST BECAUSE OF HOW I FEEL ABOUT YOU! I'M NOT SOME MINDLESS ROBOT GIRL WHO WILL JUST GO ALONG WITH EVERYTHING...

THIS IS YOUR LAST CHANCE. TELL ME THE TRUTH! YOU TWO HAVE SOME BET ABOUT ME, DON'T YOU?!

MY LAST CHANCE?

...THAT I DID THINGS THIS WAY BECAUSE I BELIEVED THAT WE REALLY TRUSTED EACH OTHER...

ARE YOU INSANE? WHY SHOULD I TRUST YOU? I HATE IT HERE, AND YOU BROUGHT ME WITHOUT ASKING... AND THEN YOU GO AROUND TELLING ME WHAT TO DO... I CAN'T STAND IT ANYMORE!

FINE! SORRY I GOT THE WRONG IDEA ABOUT US!!

I'M SORRY YOU DID, TOO!!

19

THERE ISN'T MUCH TO THIS CAMPFIRE STUFF, IS THERE? A NICE FIRE BETWEEN US WILL SET THE MOOD, HUH? HEHEHEH!

WOULD YOU QUIT IT ALREADY? THE SMOKE IS KILLING ME!

I HOPE YOU SET YOUR OWN HAIR ON FIRE, YOU MORON!

NOW, NOW, LET'S NOT BE NASTY. MAYBE YOU NEED SOME CAMPFIRE SONGS TO CHEER YOURSELVES UP...

ARE YOU KIDDING ME? WHAT ARE WE, GIRL SCOUTS?

SCOFF AWAY! I'M JANG HA-DA, THE MOOD MAKER! I'LL LIFT YOUR SPIRITS WHETHER YOU LIKE IT OR NOT!

DON'T UNDER-ESTIMATE ME!

HA-DA!! WHERE DID YOU GET THAT SNAKE?

EEEEE!!

JEEZ... I CAN'T BELIEVE HOW FAST HE GOT DRUNK!

TO HELL WITH THIS! I'VE HAD IT. I'M GOING TO SLEEP.

ㄱㅇㄴㄱ

SUN-MI... HE'S IN THE SHOWER, SO JUST SLIP IN QUIETLY AND GET UNDER THE COVERS.

GO FOR IT!!

When this is all over, I don't ever want to see this idiot again...

SHH...

THANKS!! SO-NA'S FAST ASLEEP. THE ALCOHOL MUST HAVE KNOCKED HER OUT. EVEN SO... YOU OUGHT TO PUT TAPE OVER HER MOUTH BEFORE YOU DO IT TO HER! YOU KNOW, LIKE IN THE MOVIES? HEE HEE!

25

HE'S WITH SUN-MI NOW...

OH, YOU WANT TO SCREAM ANYWAY?

GO AHEAD! THE DOOR IS LOCKED. AND EVEN IF HAE-GI COULD GET IN HERE, DON'T YOU THINK HE'D BE APPALLED TO SEE YOU LIKE THIS?

DON'T THINK YOU CAN ESCAPE THIS TIME, SO-NA!!

GET OFF OF ME, YOU BASTARD!!

DO YOU THINK YOU CAN SHAME ME INTO MARRYING YOU? DON'T BE A FOOL!

YOU'RE JUST MAKING ME HATE YOU MORE AND MORE...

OH, RELAX! STOP ACTING LIKE A SCARED LITTLE VIRGIN...

AHA!
SO I AM
YOUR FIRST.

I don't believe this! Is he really going to do this? He can't be serious! Why is this happening to me? I wish I'd never been born!!

If I scream... will Hae-Gi even come after we fought like that? And if he does break down the door...

27

스노우드롭

YOU...!!

AAGH!!

43

I'LL BE ASHAMED...

UNTIL THE DAY I CAN'T BEAT HIM BLOODY!

47

I can't handle this. I feel so sick... and I'm supposed to be getting engaged to that psycho? What did I do to deserve this life?

I don't know what to do. I feel faint, and nauseous... I can't think straight... what am I going to do about this?

Maybe I should just kill him...

DID
YOU HEAR
ME? I SAID...
I LOVE
YOU.

......

I don't know how long we sat there holding each other...

...and crying...

WHAT DID YOU SAY?!

I WON'T MARRY HWI-RIM! I DON'T CARE WHAT YOU SAY, I WON'T DO IT!

WHY THE FUSS? YOU'RE JUST NERVOUS...

YOU HAVE NO IDEA WHAT KIND OF PERSON HE REALLY IS, FATHER!

TELL ME,
THEN, WHAT KIND
OF PERSON
IS HE?

HE'S COMPLETELY
SCHIZO! HE ACTS LIKE SOME
MODEL STUDENT IN FRONT OF
YOU AND OTHER GROWN-UPS,
BUT THE REST OF THE
TIME HE'S A DISGUSTING,
PERVERTED CREEP! I'VE
NEVER MET ANYONE AS
HORRIBLE AS HIM!

THE THINGS
HE DOES -- I CAN'T
EVEN TELL YOU!
HE'S A TOTALLY
UNBALANCED
PSYCHO!!

REALLY,
SO-NA. COULD AN
"UNBALANCED PSYCHO"
BE NUMBER ONE IN
HIS CLASS?

SO-NA, YOU MUST. FOR ME...

?

YOU'RE NOT A CHILD, SO I'LL TELL YOU THE TRUTH. MY PARTY'S FUNDS ARE NOT DOING SO WELL.

I DESPERATELY NEED PRESIDENT KWON'S SUPPORT. AND DONATIONS.

IF WE DON'T GET IT, OUR POLITICAL PARTY IS GOING TO RUN INTO SERIOUS TROUBLE. AND I MAY LOSE MY POSITION.

58

THAT'S IT. GO TO YOUR ROOM.

WHAT?!

SECURITY, COME IN PLEASE

Beep

YOUR CAREER IS IMPORTANT, BUT SO IS MY LIFE!! YOU CAN'T ASK ME TO DO THIS!

I'M NOT LIKE YOU! I DON'T NEED POWER OR MONEY... OR ANYTHING!

BE QUIET. YOU'RE YOUNG. YOU HAVE NO IDEA WHAT YOU'RE TALKING ABOUT.

GET HER IN HER ROOM NOW!!

Augh!! There's no getting through to him!!

He loves me? And that's why he's selling me to help his political career?

He doesn't even care what kind of a boy he's marrying me off to!

Even if he believed me about Hwi-Rim, he wouldn't change his mind!

And anyway...

WHO GETS OFFICIALLY ENGAGED AT MY AGE?

THIS IS SO STUPID!!

MY FATHER THINKS HE CAN JUST BEND THE WORLD TO HIS WILL, AND ME ALONG WITH IT!

THERE'S ONLY ONE THING THAT I CAN DO.

I'll make sure he never tries to marry me off again...

DID YOU NEED SOMETHING, MISS?

PLEASE GET MY BODYGUARD...

I'M BORED. I WANT TO PLAY CARDS WITH HIM.

I have to talk to Hae-Gi.

Part 23.
I'll Trust You With Everything

WOWWW
~ ♡

HE'S BETTER-LOOKING EVERYTIME I SEE HIM!
~ ♡

GET A GRIP, GIRLS!! ARE YOU READY TO GO?

rude to anyone beneath her

PRETTY HOT, ISN'T IT? NOT MUCH FUN MODELING FUR IN THE SUMMER, HUH?

YOU CAN TAKE IT OFF NOW...

I'M DONE FOR TODAY, RIGHT?

65

YES, YOU'RE ALL FINISHED. MR. GARNIER COMPLIMENTED YOU TODAY, HE'S IMPRESSED WITH HOW HARD YOU WORK.

HE'D LIKE TO TREAT YOU TO DINNER.

oof, heavy

HOW'S TONIGHT?

WHAT? YEAH, THAT'S RIGHT...

TODAY IS AUGUST THIRD, RIGHT?

YOUR SUMMER BREAK IS ALMOST OVER, THAT'S WHY I THOUGHT TONIGHT WOULD BE GOOD FOR THAT DINNER...

YOU KNOW, MR. GARNIER HAS BIG PLANS FOR YOU!

WHAT?

SOME OTHER TIME. I HAVE SOMETHING TO DO TODAY.

HAE-GI!

OOH, I WAS COUNTING ON THAT DINNER TONIGHT...

MISS SO-NA!! THIS IS TOO MUCH! SERIOUSLY!

Way too much...

Way... way...

Bodyguard

...TOO MUCH! DISGUISING ME AS YOU, ASKING ME TO LEAD THE SECURITY GUARDS ON A WILD GOOSE CHASE SO YOU CAN SLIP AWAY... I CAN'T DO IT!! I WAS IN SPECIAL FORCES!!

IF I WASN'T SUCH A COWARD, I COULD HAVE BECOME AN OPERATIVE FOR THE GOVERNMENT!

BUT THIS? DRESSING AS A GIRL?

OH, PLEASE!

SHUT UP! THEY'LL HEAR YOU!

AAGH!!

DO YOU WANT TO JUST STAND BY AND WATCH ME DIE? THIS IS MY LAST REQUEST OF YOU. WE'VE BEEN TOGETHER EVERY DAY FOR SO LONG, DOESN'T THAT MEAN ANYTHING TO YOU?

I WON'T FORGET THIS KINDNESS!

Okay, okay...

THANK YOU.

NOW -- OPEN THE DOOR, AND THEN RUN LIKE HELL TOWARD THE GATE.

MISS!! STOP!!

QUICK, AFTER HER!!

HA HA, IT'S WORKING!

STUPID GUARDS, I CAN'T BELIEVE THEY WERE FOOLED SO EASILY...

수르륵

TOO BAD FATHER DOESN'T KNOW I'VE BEEN DOING THIS FOR YEARS

JUST GOT TO GET OVER THE FENCE...

This could be the very last time I do this...

The last time I see our nursery...

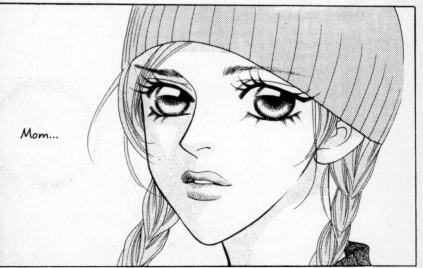

Mom...

SO-NA!

I'LL DO ANYTHING TO HELP YOU SO-NA. YOU KNOW THAT.

I don't need anything from my father...

I'M SO PROUD! I CAN'T BELIEVE MY GRANDSON IS GETTING ENGAGED ALREADY.

HMPH.

These idiots! All they care about is the deal they've made with the Yu family. They haven't even seen So-Na, they don't know what she's like...or care. Do they still think she's really going to go through with this?

?

I ONLY MET SO-NA ONCE, BUT I'M THRILLED THAT SHE WILL BE JOINING OUR FAMILY.

75

Now we enter a new chapter.

WHAT A WONDERFUL DAY FOR ALL OF US!

HA HA! YES! I'M SO HAPPY YOU'RE TAKING SO-NA INTO YOUR FAMILY. I TRUST SHE'LL DO YOU PROUD!

I'M SURE SHE WILL! I HEAR THAT SHE IS A VERY SMART AND CLEVER GIRL.

I can't believe she came to the engagement ceremony. What's going on? After what I did? So-Na...does money come before honor for you, too?

No. I don't believe it. Not for money, or politics. You're stronger than I thought...

What could you be up to?

She being so calm and quiet...it's totally unlike her. I know she couldn't have changed her mind so quickly. So what is she doing?

A NICE QUIET PARTY LIKE THIS IS PERFECT FOR AN ENGAGEMENT, ISN'T IT?

WITH THE ECONOMY THE WAY IT IS, IT'S GOOD TO JUST HAVE A SMALL DINNER...

PLEASE EXCHANGE THE RINGS OF BETROTHAL!

I'M SO PROUD!

EVERYTHING IS JUST PERFECT. I HOPE YOU TWO BECOME GOOD FRIENDS AND LIVE HAPPILY EVER AFTER...

THANK YOU VERY MUCH.

WHAT A BUNCH OF HYPOCRITES. EVERYONE HERE KNOWS THIS IS A BUSINESS DEAL, WITH SO-NA AS THE CURRENCY...

NO. WE WON'T BECOME GOOD FRIENDS.

WE WILL NOT GET MARRIED, OR ENGAGED!

84

85

NOTHING AT ALL. JUST TRY AND STOP ME NOW.

Don't cry...don't cry...

I might have gone
too far but -- I had no other
way out. I'm not ashamed. At
least I'm on a path of my own
choosing, for the first time
in my life.

My life won't be easy after this. I'll have to face the world on my own.

But I'll never regret it!

art 24: Glass Castles

HEY, HWI-RIM!
WE HEAR YOU'RE
GOING TO MARRY THE
CONGRESSMAN'S
DAUGHTER!

DO YOU THINK HE REALLY WANTS THE SON OF A WHORE TO TAKE OVER?

LOOK AT HER, CARRYING BOOKS AROUND AS IF SHE ACTUALLY GETS GOOD GRADES.

HEE! HEE! HEE!

BUT AT LEAST SHE'S AN HEIRESS.

GOOD LUCK, HWI-RIM. FROM WHAT I HEAR, THAT GIRL IS TROUBLE.

I hate this family. The abuse I take from them—it never stops.

My father died very young, before I was born. My mother was his favorite call girl... She took money from my grandfather and then dumped me here and vanished. My grandfather told me that she only got pregnant to extort money from him anyway.

I can't even remember how many times I got locked in the attic, or went without food. They were always sayin'

"Little bastard!"
"Son of a whore!"

THIS IS THE BEST I COULD GET WITH THE MONEY I HAD.

IT'S NOT MUCH TO LOOK AT. AND I DIDN'T HAVE A CHANCE TO BUY YOU FOOD, BUT...

WHAT DID THIS COST?

NEXT MONTH WHEN I GET PAID, WE'LL FIND YOU A NICER PLACE.

WHEN YOU GET PAID? I'M GOING TO EARN MY OWN MONEY!!

I KNOW I DON'T HAVE ANYTHING RIGHT NOW, BUT I'M GOING TO PAY YOU BACK EVERY PENNY.

IF YOU'RE SUPPORTING ME, THAT DEFEATS THE WHOLE PURPOSE OF MY LEAVING HOME!!

THANK YOU...

BUT DON'T TRY TO HELP ME OUT AFTER THIS. I WANT TO DO THIS ON MY OWN. I MEAN IT. TAKING HELP FROM YOU...

NOW YOU KNOW HOW I FELT.

WHEN YOU WANTED TO HELP ME, IT MADE ME VERY UNCOMFORTABLE.

I COULDN'T OFFER YOU ANYTHING IN RETURN...EXCEPT MY BODY...

I WASN'T ASKING FOR ANYTHING IN RETURN!! I JUST WANTED TO--

SO-NA...I FEEL THE SAME WAY YOU DID.

WE BOTH KNOW HOW WE FEEL...

ALL RIGHT... LET'S PROMISE TO BE HONEST WITH EACH OTHER. IF WE NEED HELP, IF WE'RE IN TROUBLE, WE'LL TELL EACH OTHER. OKAY?

ARE YOU SURE THIS IS OKAY? WON'T YOUR FATHER BE WORRIED?

DON'T WORRY ABOUT HIM. MY FATHER IS A MAN WHO IS MORE SCARY THAN YOU CAN IMAGINE.

WHAT DO YOU MEAN, "SCARY"? HOW SO?

TRUST ME. HE JUST IS...

103

SO YOU REALLY THOUGHT I WAS JUST A SPOILED LITTLE PRINCESS WHEN WE FIRST MET?

HA HA! TOTALLY! THE WAY YOU ALWAYS HAVE YOUR NOSE IN THE AIR?

LIKE YOU'RE THINKING, "HOW DARE YOU EVEN LOOK AT ME!"

OH, REALLY? WELL I THOUGHT YOU WERE JUST A DULL AND SIMPLE BOY...

WELL, I THINK I'M PRETTY SIMPLE...I'M AN OPEN BOOK!

YOU'RE SIMPLE? I'VE NEVER EVEN HAD A BOYFRIEND BEFORE!

REALLY? I'M YOUR FIRST?

......

HEY, IT'S GETTING LATE, ISN'T IT? YOU SHOULD GET GOING!

NOT UNTIL YOU'RE SAFELY ASLEEP. DON'T WORRY ABOUT ME, JUST TRY AND RELAX...

Easily broken, and sometimes sharp...castles of glass who end up hurting ourselves.

But our fragility is what makes us beautiful.

SIR, HERE'S T
REPORT ON TH
BOY YOU HAD
INVESTIGAT

HE'S A CLASSMATE OF MISS SO-NA'S. AND A MODEL.

SHE LEFT THE PARTY WITH HIM. DON'T WORRY, THEY NEVER SAW US FOLLOWING THEM.

Has my daughter really grown up?

JUST LEAVE IT THERE.

...

So-Na, the world is such a hard place. Why do you keep trying to fight it? Why must you always take the hardest path?

After everything you've suffered in your short life... why do you keep struggling?

This is a hard world for a woman like you. I wanted to see you safely taken into a good family, but...

109

Ooh! It's like we're newlyweds! ♡♡

오ㅅ

짝 쭉

Get a grip, So-Na! I didn't leave home to act like a silly schoolgirl!

What time is it, anyway?

10 o'clock! I overslept! I'm such a loser!

I'm on my own from now on. I've got to earn my own money, and solve my own problems...

I'll have to become a success without any help. Look out world! Here I come!!

LET'S EAT FAST FOOD

꼬르륵

꼬

Hmm. After I eat, that is.

No, I can't just eat fast food.

113

THE MARKETPLACE

HEY! GET YOUR OWN PAPER!

I'M BROKE.

What? It's a free paper! Is she stupid? Is she making fun of me?

HEH HEH.. I GOT HER COPY.

BUT CAN'T CALL ANYBODY!

I USED MY LAST BIT OF CHANGE TO GET A DRINK!

WHAT KIND OF AN IDIOT AM I? I DON'T BELIEVE THIS!

I'm just a bum! Who's starving!

HELP WANTED STARTING IMMEDIATELY

116

I've been to so many places today.

I've been looking for hours, and I haven't earned a penny. This is so much harder than I imagined. What am I going to do?

Everyone says I'm too young.

30 MINUTES FREE IN OUR KARAOKE ROOM!

I can't even afford to die.

Is 17 really so young?

HEY! WAIT UP!

Does he mean me?

HAS ANYONE EVER TOLD YOU THAT YOU MAKE A GOOD IMPRESSION?

What? No one's ever said anything like that to me. Who is this guy?

I WAS WONDERING... WOULD YOU BE INTERESTED IN WORKING AT MY PLACE?

A job?

Wait. This is suspicious! He seems nice, but what if he's a kidnapper! Or a pimp! I'd better make sure...

JUST WHAT KIND OF PLACE CAN HIRE MINORS? I'M A 17-YEAR-OLD RUNAWAY, WITH NO LEGAL GUARDIAN, AND I'M JUST WARNING YOU, IF THIS IS SOMETHING THAT WILL BREAK THE "TEENAGERS PROTECTION LAW"...

YOU COULD GET THREE YEARS IN PRISON, AND PAY HUGE FINES!

Who should
I call?

Hae-Gi...

YOU HAVE
GOT TO BE
KIDDING!!

YOU'RE A RIOT, SO-NA!! WHAT WERE YOU THINKING? YOU RAN AWAY FROM HOME WITH NOTHING?

I'm so hungry, I'll even take this abuse...

AND AFTER WALKING OUT ON YOUR ENGAGEMENT SO PROUDLY!

ALTHOUGH, DIDN'T YOUR DAD PAY FOR YOUR BRA AND PANTIES, TOO?

IF ONLY I COULD HAVE SEEN IT--

SHUT UP, HA-DA!

HA HA HA HA! YOU'RE REALLY SOMETHING, SO-NA. I'VE NEVER HEARD OF A KID MAKING SUCH A MESS OUT OF REBELLING. IT'S JUST TOO MUCH!

AND THAT BASTARD HWI-RIM, HE CAN'T EVEN SHOW HIS FACE IN PUBLIC AFTER WHAT YOU DID TO HIM. HA!

YOU'VE MADE YOUR POINT, THOUGH. AREN'T YOU READY TO GO BACK HOME YET?

122

I WAS WORRIED ABOUT YOU TOO, YOU KNOW.

I'VE BEEN LOOKING FOR YOU ALL DAY. THANK GOD YOU CALLED ME. C'MON, I'LL TAKE YOU BACK HOME. NOW THAT YOU'VE SHOWN YOUR DAD HOW YOU FEEL--

I'M NOT GOING BACK.

MAYBE I FAILED TODAY.

BUT TOMORROW I WILL GET A JOB. AND IF I DON'T, I'LL KEEP TRYING UNTIL I DO! I DIDN'T RUN AWAY FOR FUN, OR TO SCARE MY FATHER. I'VE DECIDED TO FINALLY BECOME INDEPENDENT!

ARE YOU INSANE?

YES! I'VE GONE NUTS! SO YOU'D BETTER PAY ME BACK EVERY CENT YOU'VE EVER BORROWED!

THAT'S WHY I CALLED YOU! TO GET MY MONEY BACK!

ALL YOU TALK ABOUT IS MONEY, MONEY, MONEY...

OH, SHUT UP! AFTER TODAY, I REALIZE THAT MONEY IS ALL THAT MATTERS IN THIS WORLD. SO HAND IT OVER, ALREADY!

TRY STARVING ALL DAY AND SEE HOW YOU LIKE IT! TRY WORRYING ABOUT WHAT YOU'LL EAT TOMORROW!

AND NOW IT'S FOOD, FOOD, FOOD...

HAE-GI!

THANKS FOR TAKING CARE OF THE IDIOT GIRL! I JUST CAME TO SEE WHERE SHE'S STAYING, SO DON'T GET ANY WRONG IDEAS.

BE QUIET! THIS IS MY HOME, AND YOU'RE MY FRIEND WHO'S VISITING, THAT'S ALL!

YOU'RE BOTH MY FRIENDS!

SHE CALLED ME BECAUSE SHE WAS HUNGRY. WONDER WHY SHE DIDN'T CALL YOU?

127

HER? AN ATHLETE'S-FOOT MODEL, MAYBE...

THERE'S A SHOW COMING UP AND THEY WANT A BRAND-NEW MODEL FOR IT. OF COURSE, YOU'LL HAVE TO AUDITION, BUT...

...IF YOU MODEL, YOU CAN STILL GO TO SCHOOL, AND THE PAY'S GOOD ENOUGH THAT YOU DON'T HAVE TO WORRY ABOUT PAYING YOUR BILLS.

UT I WANT O MAKE IT WITHOUT OUR HELP!

DON'T BE STUPID!! MODELING IS 100 PERCENT ABOUT YOUR ABILITY. I CAN'T DO ANYTHING TO HELP YOU GET THE JOB.

HEY, SO-NA, IF IT'S A JOB HAE-GI CAN MANAGE, YOU COULD DO IT, EASY! AND YOU'VE BEEN APPROACHED BY TALENT SCOUTS A BUNCH OF TIMES, REMEMBER?

YOU'RE TALL, PRETTY, AND YOUR LEGS ARE AWESOME. OF COURSE, YOUR CHEST IS AS FLAT AS A BOARD BUT...

129

DON'T YOU THINK IT'S TIME YOU GOT GOING, HA-DA?

Modeling?

RIGHT. AND LEAVE YOU HERE TO TAKE CARE OF HER? SOME JOB YOU'VE DONE SO FAR!

I'd never even considered it. If my father finds out, he'd be so angry. Being famous means...

...lots of money!

OKAY! I CAN DO IT!

Suddenly, I see a glimmer of hope.

"I can do it"? Don't you mean, "I'll try"?

Rice?

I'LL BE ABLE TO DO IT! I'L... MAKE MY OWN W... IN THIS WORLD. GOING TO EARN... TON OF MONEY... BUY LOTS OF R...

130

AND THAT'S IT FOR TODAY.

HA HA. SHE PICKED CHANGE UP OFF THE STREET?

I THINK SHE MAY BE LEARNING SOME VALUABLE LESSONS.

SIR...HOW LONG ARE YOU GOING TO JUST STAND BY AND WATCH HER?

IF SHE WERE A BOY, IT WOULD BE ONE THING TO LET HER LIVE ON THE STREETS AND GET AN EDUCATION ABOUT REAL LIFE BUT AS A GIRL....

AS A GIRL? SHE HAS NO CHANCE AS A GIRL, NOW. NO FAMILY WILL ACCEPT HER AFTER WHAT HAPPENED.

THE RUMORS HAVE SPREAD ALREADY. NO ONE WILL WANT HER FOR A DAUGHTER-IN-LAW. MY ONLY CHOICE IS TO START TREATING HER LIKE A SON.

I'M GOING TO LET HER TASTE THE BITTERNESS OF THE WORLD A LITTLE MORE...AND THEN BRING HER BACK IN.

THEN WE'LL START GROOMING HER TO SUCCEED ME AS HEAD OF OUR PARTY SOMEDAY! NOW THAT I KNOW WHAT SO-NA WANTS, I KNOW WHAT TO DO WITH HER!

YOU'RE...NOT ANGRY WITH HER?

HA HA! HOW COULD I BE, WHEN SHE'S JUST LIKE ME?

she's great!

JUST WATCH OVER HER...AND MAKE SURE SHE NEVER FINDS OUT ABOUT YOU.

YES, SIR.

OH, HAVE YOU READ THE FILE I PREPARED?

ABOUT THE BOY SHE'S SEEING. OH HAE-GI...

OH, THIS

WAIT...WHAT DID YOU SAY HIS NAME WAS?

오 해기
......

OH HAE-GI...

NO. SHE HAS NO CHANCE.

WHAT?

SHE'S TOO STUCK-UP.

HER EYES... SHE LOOKS LIKE SHE THINKS SHE'S ABOVE EVERYONE ELSE. WHAT DO YOU WANT TO BE A MODEL FOR, ANYWAY?

Is he serious?

FOR THE MONEY, RIGHT? TSK.

OH, LIKE YOU'RE WORKING FOR FREE? WITH ALL YOUR LAME EXPENSIVE DESIGNER LABELS... NO ONE IN THIS WORLD WORKS WITHOUT GETTING PAID, POPS--

OH, MAN. I DID IT AGAIN.

WHAT'S WRONG WITH ME? WHY CAN'T I CONTROL MYSELF? AND I CALLED HIM "POPS"? I DESERVE WHATEVER I GET...

WHAT AM I GOING TO DO, HAE-GI?

LISTEN TO ME, SO-NA. YOU HAVE A CHOICE.

134

IF YOU DON'T WANT TO WORK, I'LL SUPPORT YOU. I'M FINE WITH THAT.

BUT IF YOU REALLY WANT TO BE INDEPENDENT, YOU NEED TO GO IN THERE, APOLOGIZE AND BEG FOR A JOB.

EXCUSE ME...
OH HAE-GI?

WE'D
LIKE TO TALK
TO YOU.

WHAT?

JUST SHUT
UP AND COME
ALONG!

스노우
드롭

YOU'RE VERY YOUNG... WHAT DID THEY SAY? 17?

143

I'LL TRANSFER PLENTY OF MONEY INTO YOUR ACCOUNT, SO YOU WON'T HAVE ANY TROUBLE STARTING OVER AGAIN. BUT YOU NEED TO DO WHAT I SAY...

WHAT?

OR ELSE... YOU ARE DEAD.

AND DON'T THINK I'M BLUFFING, BOY. WE COULD KILL YOU RIGHT HERE, AND NO ONE WOULD EVER KNOW. I'M NOT JOKING AROUND HERE.

THE POLICE HAVE A LOT MORE TO WORRY ABOUT THAN THE DEATH OF ONE USELESS TEENAGER. END THINGS WITH SO-NA. NOW. YOU HAVE NO IDEA WHAT KIND OF DANGER YOU ARE IN.

THERE'S MORE GOING ON HERE THAN YOU CAN POSSIBLY UNDERSTAND. NO MATTER HOW YOU FEEL ABOUT IT, TRUST ME. DON'T THINK ABOUT IT. END IT. NOW.

DO WE UNDERSTAND EACH OTHER? GOOD. I'M GIVING YOU ONE WEEK TO GET YOUR FAMILY OUT OF TOWN!

I WON'T!!

GIVE ME ONE GOOD REASON I SHOULD LEAVE! I MAY BE A NOBODY NOW, BUT...

...SOMEDAY, I'M GOING TO BECOME A MAN WORTHY OF SO-NA! AND I MADE HER A PROMISE, TO ALWAYS BE BY HER SIDE. EVEN IF IT COSTS ME MY LIFE, I WON'T BREAK THAT PROMISE!

YOU CAN'T MAKE ME RUN AWAY FROM MY LIFE! I DON'T CARE WHAT YOU SAY! FORGET IT!

STUBBORN, AREN'T YOU?

149

YOU WANT ME TO CLEAN ALL THIS UP?

THAT'S RIGHT.

...

DO MODELS USUALLY DO STUFF LIKE THIS?

WHO SAYS YOU A MODE

YOU'RE JUST A LOWLY ASSISTANT.

!?

THEN WHY DID I HAVE TO TRY OUT?

BECAUSE!

NO MATTER WHAT THE JOB IS, I WON'T HAVE ANYONE WORKING HERE UNLESS THEY'VE GOT STYLE.

WHO DOES HE THINK HE IS?

DOES HE THINK I'M AN IDIOT?

DAMN IT!

SELFISH BASTARD! JERKING ME AROUND LIKE THAT!

IF YOU DON'T WANT TO DO IT, THEN QUIT.

cursing out, eh

AH...IT'S OKAY. I DIDN'T REALLY WANT TO BE A MODEL. I HATE DIETING.

GOOD. THEN GET TO WORK!

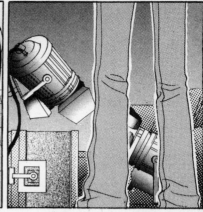

HERE GOES!

The truth is, I'd rather be doing stuff like this than modeling.

Standing in front of people like that...it's too creepy! I'll start from the bottom and work my way up to a really good job! Everyone has to start somewhere!

DID YOU PERM YOUR HAIR?

PRETTY FASHIONABLE, HUH? I'M LUCKY TO WORK AT SUCH A GREAT SALON.

A REALLY FAMOUS STYLIST SAID HE'LL TRAIN ME! THE PAY IS GREAT, AND AS A BONUS, HE ASKED ME TO WEAR STUFF FROM HIS CLOTHING LINE BECAUSE I WEAR THEM SO WELL!

THEY'RE CUTE, HUH?

TOTALLY! AND THEY'RE SO YOU!!

Thanks!

Caught themselves talking like they're still dating.

153

AHEM. I WANTED TO TALK TO YOU...TO ASK WHAT KIND OF A GUY ACTS LIKE A GIRL. YOU NEED TO GET YOUR ACT TOGETHER, OBVIOUSLY THERE'S SOMETHING WRONG WITH YOU...

WHAT?

WRONG WITH ME?

YEAH! THAT'S RIGHT! LOOK AT ALL THE TROUBLE YOU'VE CAUSED! YOU NEED HELP!

HEE HEE HEE!!

YOU'RE THE ONE THE NEEDS HELP!! WHO'S THE ONE WHO FELL FOR ME, HUH?

DON'T UNDERESTIMATE ME, HA-DA.

Experience?

DID HE JUST INSULT ME?

NO MATTER HOW I LOOK, I'M MORE POPULAR WITH GIRLS THAN MOST GUYS. AND I'VE HAD MORE EXPERIENCE, TOO...

DAMN IT!

STOP ACTING SO SUPERIOR! AND WHILE YOU'RE AT IT, STOP BOTHERING ME ALREADY!

YOU'RE THE ONE WHO'S ACTING SUPERIOR!

WHY DID YOU LIE TO ME, KO-MO? WHY DID YOU SAY YOU WERE A GIRL?

THEN...

WHAT ARE YOU GOING TO DO?

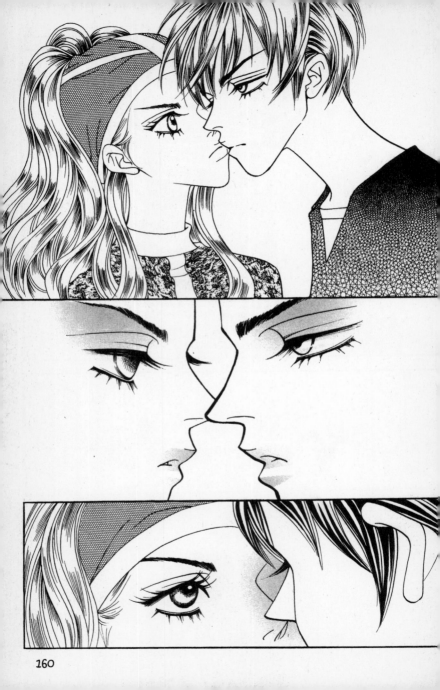

WHAT ARE YOU, CRAZY?

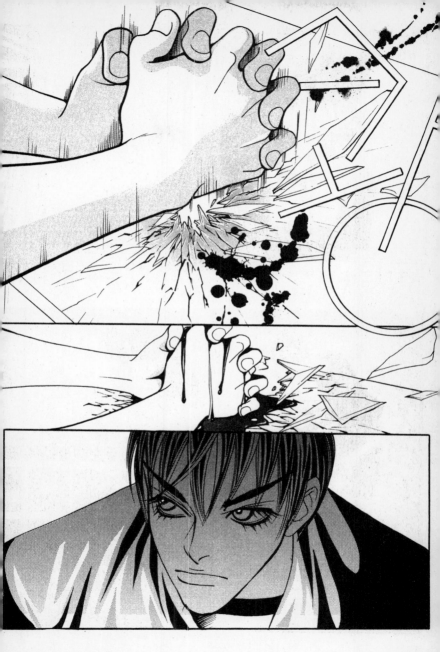

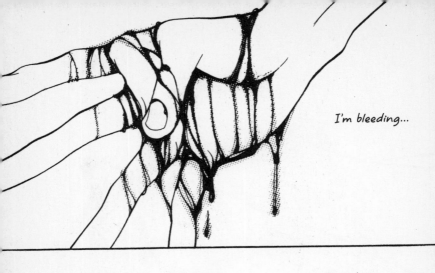

I'm bleeding...

Who cares?

Damn him.

Why?
Why do I like
him so?

From the Studio! A Snow Drop Parody.

S.O... Snow Drop - Special Edition

CHOI HERE!! I'VE COME THIS FAR BECAUSE OF ALL YOUR LOVE AND SUPPORT...

AND NOW, TO REPAY YOU, I BRING YOU THIS SPECIAL VERSION OF SNOW DROP! JUST RELAX, SUSPEND DISBELIEF AND GO ALONG FOR THE RIDE...

READY?

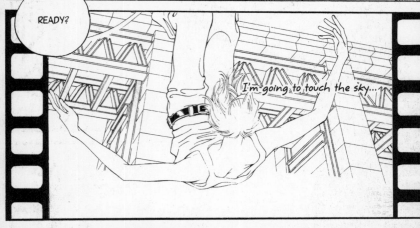

I'm going to touch the sky...

That stream was really just 20" deep!!

KLONK!!

OWW...IT'S SO PAINFUL WORKING TO SUPPORT YOUR FAMILY.

IT HURTS ME MORE THAN YOU!!

And now... Jang Ha-Da, on the prowl!!!

167

Still, Ko-Mo being a boy is a problem for Ha-Da. Once ...

ROMANCE COMICS ARE ALWAYS GOING ON ABOUT LOVE...

HEY, HA-DA...WHY ARE YOU READING A GAY ROMANCE COMIC?

WHAT?

tsk

I DON'T KNOW WHY I LIKE YOU...

THIS ISN'T EASY...

WHY?

WHO CARES ABOUT GIRLS?

OH!!

AH!

I'M NOT LIKE THAT!!

Ha-Da goes into shock!! He thinks it's completely ridiculous, but...he feels the sting of truth...

His love toward Ko-Mo is...

I NEED TO KNOW... WHAT DOES IT MEAN TO LIKE ANOTHER MAN?

Oh.

Oh.

Oh.

This book says love has no borders. I don't understand my heart. I think love is a terrible, fickle, butterfly...

Suddenly, Ha-Da becomes deep...

I LOVE YOU...

HEH.

I DON'T KNOW WHAT MADE ME LOVE YOU, BUT...NOW I CAN'T LIVE WITHOUT YOU...

I'M NOT THE JANG HA-DA I USED TO BE...

I CAN'T HELP MYSELF!! I LOVE YOU!

Cosmos flower* →

DO YOU HAVE TO MAKE SUCH A FUSS?

SERIOUSLY IT'S SO ANNOYING.

This is Ha-Da being shy...

*Note: Ko-Mo was named after the Cosmos flower that Ha-Da is offering hir

170

And here's So-Na, persecuted by Kwon Hwi-Rim.

HWI-RIM!!

IT'S YOU! ARE YOU GIVING IN TO ME AT LAST?

HEH! LOVE THE COSTUME!

GOOD CHOICE, SINCE I'M THE ONLY ONE WHO CAN MAKE YOU A QUEEN!

IN THE NAME OF THE GODS OF ROMANTIC COMEDY, I WILL PUNISH YOU! THE GODS GIVE ME POWER!

HOW DARE YOU DISRESPECT ME!! DIE, YOU FOOL!

KEEP GOING! I LOVE IT!

Uh oh! The evil king Hwi-Rim transforms into a villain!

So what!! An eye for an eye, that's what I say!! He's burned me up so bad I gotta kick him around to cool down! After all, I have the power of the gods of romantic comedy!

TAKE THAT!

HEE-YAH!!

She's wiping him out to his very core...

BASTARD!

FLOP

THAT WAS TOO CRUEL!!

LOOK WHAT YOU DID!!

I SUFFERED LIKE SHE DID, TOO, SINCE I WAS TRAPPED IN A ROMANTIC COMEDY, I COULDN'T DO ANYTHING BUT CRY, IN FRONT OF BACKGROUNDS FULL OF FLOWERS...

He's been reduced to a stick figure!!

Wha??

What?

173

And the ghosts of the haunted mansion?

The little girl...

The owner...

The scary girl...

They are a family that lived in the haunted inn.

Dad

KIDS! I KNOW HOW WE CAN IMPROVE OUR BUSINESS!

little sis

YAY!!

WE CAN DO IT!

older sis

They decided to turn their bizarre looks to their advantage and act like ghosts.

They even installed the latest in SFX technology

174

차르르

Hidden behind the curtain was a special projector that made the image.

Hee hee! It cost big money!!

She successfully frightened them, but...

IT WORKED!! THEY'RE TOTALLY SCARED...THEY'LL TELL EVERYONE BACK HOME, PEOPLE WILL COME AND WE'LL BE RICH!!

YAY!

HO HO HO. NEXT, I'LL WEAR THIS AND SCARE THEM EVEN MORE...

I'LL KILL YOU!

AAAH!!

YOU'RE DEAD, HWI-RIM!!

HAE-GI! YOU'RE REALLY GOING TO KILL HIM! STOP!!

YOU LIKE LIVING DANGEROUSLY, DON'T YOU...?

You three are scarier.

LET'S GO! I CAN'T STAND TO BE AROUND THEM FOR EVEN ONE MORE SECOND.

we're scared...

BUT WE NEVER FOUND OUT...ARE THERE REALLY GHOSTS HERE?

DAMN IT, HA-DA, WHO CARES?

...but their dream was destroyed.

They gave it their best effort ...

Goodbye...

175

Once upon a time, there lived a princess. She had a malicious disposition and an IQ below 90.

She also had a magical mirror that talked.

MIRROR, MIRROR ON THE WALL, WHO'S THE PRETTIEST OF THEM ALL?

OOH LA LA!

YU SO-NA OF ZEE NEXT COUNTRY EES THE PRETTIEST OF ZEM ALL!

WHAT DID YOU SAY?!

HOW DARE YOU?!

파창

EET WAS A JOKE, MY PREENCESS!!

PRINCESS YU SO-NA? ALL I HAVE TO DO IS DISPOSE OF YOU, THEN I'LL BE PRETTIEST OF THEM ALL!

No one said she was 2nd place...

So she dresses as a witch and learns black magic!!

OH, MY DEAR! I BRING YOU THIS APPLE. IT WILL CURE YOUR HORRIBLE GAS AND DIARRHEA!

JUST ONE BITE...

HOW DARE YOU SPEAK TO ME THAT WAY?

THAT'S NOT HOW THE STORY GOES, ANYWAY.

SHE'S NOT PRETTIER THAN ME!!

One lazy afternoon...

So-Na asks Hae-Gi to go and study with her. But she can't stop sneaking looks at him...

He's asleep.

Look at those lashes, he's so gorgeous...

I wonder what he's dreaming about? Is it a fun dream? A nightmare? Or a dream about...

us?

HUH? I FELL ASLEEP...

I'm late! So late!!

WHAT? WHO ARE YOU? QUICK, SPEAK UP!!

HUH?

AM I STILL ASLEEP?

I FEEL LIKE ALICE IN WONDERLAND...

I'm busy busy busy!

HEY, YOU, TELL ME WHAT HAPPENS NEXT!

I don't remember!

Here's poor Sun-Mi. No one loves her, not even the readers. So sad...

쿨럭 쿨럭

OH, WOE IS ME! NOBODY LOVES ME!

And Charles, another lonely soul...

휘오오

IT'S...SO... COLD...

They feel they've been wronged by the world around them!

YOU TOO?

ME TOO!

Two lonely souls understand each other, and a love blossoms...

A FORBIDDEN LOVE!

NO WAY!!

179

HEY GUYS! I HOPE YOU ALL ENJOYED THIS. I WANTED TO PUT EVEN MORE JOKES INTO IT BUT...

THEY'LL HAVE TO WAIT UNTIL THE NEXT TIME!! HEE HEE!

THE SPECIAL VERSION WAS PRETTY COOL, HUH? I TRIED TO PUT IN SOME OF MY DIFFERENT IDEAS ABOUT SNOW DROP AND SOME OF THE FUNNY THINGS I THOUGHT OF!

I LIKED DOING A COMEDY VERSION.

SOMETIMES, THE EXTRAS IN A BOOK CAN BE TH MOST FUN, DON'T YOU THINK?

OH, SOME NEW ASSISTANTS HAVE JOINED MY STUDIO! I'D LIKE YOU TO MEET THEM.

KIDS, SAY HELLO!

HI!! I'M JUNG BO-EUN, AND I'M THE REAL LEADER OF THE STUDIO, HO HO HO!

HEWWO DERE!! I'M JANG SOO-JIN! I'M THE BLACK SHEEP OF THE FAMILY...

called the lying soprano

called rubber gloves

I'M YIM JUNG-JIN! AND COMICS ARE MY ONE TRUE LOVE!

LEAVE THIS COUNTRY'S COMICS UNDER MY PROTECTION!

CREATION IS FREEING! AND WE LONG TO DO IT!

COMICS, I WILL LOVE YOU FOR THE REST OF MY LIFE!!

WHEN I THINK ABOUT IT, A LOT HAS HAPPENED THIS YEAR.

I got married, and then my son Ji-Ho was born. Those were my big events!!

I BET YOU'RE ALL WONDERING WHAT JI-HO LOOKS LIKE, HUH?

HERE HE IS!

SAY HELLO, JI-HO!

Snow Drop Volume 6 **The End**

Coming in January

Volume Seven

In a startling disclosure,
So-Na's father tells Hae-Gi
and So-Na the real reason
why he doesn't want them
to be with each other.
Unfazed, Hae-Gi secretly
tries to talk to So-Na. When
So-Na's father discovers
them together, he pulls out a
gun and gives Hae-Gi an
ultimatum. What will the
forbidden lovers do? Hold
your breath and don't
reveal the surprise twists
and turns--this volume of
Snow Drop will have to be
read and reread to be
believed!

**Drop in for
SNOW DROP Volume 7!**

IN THE BATTLE OF THE BANDS,
HIS VOICE IS
THE ULTIMATE WEAPON!

DRAGON VOICE
™

A touching story about a regular guy with an irregular gift.

HANDS OFF!

www.TOKYOPO

T TEEN AGE 13+

forbidden Dance ™

by Hinako Ashihara

Dancing was her life...

Her dance partner
might be her future...

Available Now

ALSO AVAILABLE FROM  TOKYOPOP®

MANGA

.HACK//LEGEND OF THE TWILIGHT
@LARGE
ABENOBASHI: MAGICAL SHOPPING ARCADE
A.I. LOVE YOU
AI YORI AOSHI
ANGELIC LAYER
ARM OF KANNON
BABY BIRTH
BATTLE ROYALE
BATTLE VIXENS
BOYS BE...
BRAIN POWERED
BRIGADOON
B'TX
CANDIDATE FOR GODDESS, THE
CARDCAPTOR SAKURA
CARDCAPTOR SAKURA - MASTER OF THE CLOW
CHOBITS
CHRONICLES OF THE CURSED SWORD
CLAMP SCHOOL DETECTIVES
CLOVER
COMIC PARTY
CONFIDENTIAL CONFESSIONS
CORRECTOR YUI
COWBOY BEBOP
COWBOY BEBOP: SHOOTING STAR
CRAZY LOVE STORY
CRESCENT MOON
CROSS
CULDCEPT
CYBORG 009
D•N•ANGEL
DEMON DIARY
DEMON ORORON, THE
DEUS VITAE
DIABOLO
DIGIMON
DIGIMON TAMERS
DIGIMON ZERO TWO
DOLL
DRAGON HUNTER
DRAGON KNIGHTS
DRAGON VOICE
DREAM SAGA
DUKLYON: CLAMP SCHOOL DEFENDERS
EERIE QUEERIE!
ERICA SAKURAZAWA: COLLECTED WORKS
ET CETERA
ETERNITY
EVIL'S RETURN
FAERIES' LANDING
FAKE
FLCL
FLOWER OF THE DEEP SLEEP, THE
FORBIDDEN DANCE
FRUITS BASKET

G GUNDAM
GATEKEEPERS
GETBACKERS
GIRL GOT GAME
GRAVITATION
GTO
GUNDAM SEED ASTRAY
GUNDAM WING
GUNDAM WING: BATTLEFIELD OF PACIFISTS
GUNDAM WING: ENDLESS WALTZ
GUNDAM WING: THE LAST OUTPOST (G-UNIT)
HANDS OFF!
HAPPY MANIA
HARLEM BEAT
HYPER RUNE
I.N.V.U.
IMMORTAL RAIN
INITIAL D
INSTANT TEEN: JUST ADD NUTS
ISLAND
JING: KING OF BANDITS
JING: KING OF BANDITS - TWILIGHT TALES
JULINE
KARE KANO
KILL ME, KISS ME
KINDAICHI CASE FILES, THE
KING OF HELL
KODOCHA: SANA'S STAGE
LAMENT OF THE LAMB
LEGAL DRUG
LEGEND OF CHUN HYANG, THE
LES BIJOUX
LOVE HINA
LOVE OR MONEY
LUPIN III
LUPIN III: WORLD'S MOST WANTED
MAGIC KNIGHT RAYEARTH I
MAGIC KNIGHT RAYEARTH II
MAHOROMATIC: AUTOMATIC MAIDEN
MAN OF MANY FACES
MARMALADE BOY
MARS
MARS: HORSE WITH NO NAME
MINK
MIRACLE GIRLS
MIYUKI-CHAN IN WONDERLAND
MODEL
MOURYOU KIDEN: LEGEND OF THE NYMPHS
NECK AND NECK
ONE
ONE I LOVE, THE
PARADISE KISS
PARASYTE
PASSION FRUIT
PEACH GIRL
PEACH GIRL: CHANGE OF HEART
PET SHOP OF HORRORS
PITA-TEN

07.15.04T

LEGAL DRUG ™

When no ordinary prescription will do...

FROM CLAMP CREATORS OF CHOBITS & TOKYO BABYLON